WHAT READERS ARE SAYING

"This book is a life changing must-read for those in passionate pursuit of how to stop procrastination"
-**Karen Weber,** *Germany*

"This book showed me how much self-doubt affects every area of my life. The book encouraged me, equipped me, and changed me. Honestly, I think everyone should read it"
-*Joshua Barns, California*

"This book gave me courage and clarification to believe in myself"
-*Segun Adebayo, Nigeria*

"In all my forty-five years, I've never read a book that spoke to me, moved me, and set me free from so many issues. I couldn't put it down!"
-*Michael Kwame, Ghana*

"For as long as I've known Adeola Babatunde, he has been energised by his purpose and passion – and engaged with a worthy vision, knowing he has test-driven each of his chapters, I found myself deeply open to his wisdom and encouragement. Adeola brings not only information; he brings himself and those test-driven convictions-personally, vulnerably and clearly"
-*Albert Anderson, London*

Acknowledgement

Special thanks to my wife (Bola) and Children (David, Daniel and Debbie) who gave me the time and space to write.

To the Authors and Teachers I have learnt from, for their guidance and support along the way.

To my clients who allowed me to share what I have learnt through relating with them.

===

All rights reserved. No part of this publication may be reproduced, stored in a retrieval system, or transmitted, in any form or by any means without the prior permission in writing of the author or as expressly permitted by law, or under terms agreed with the appropriate reprographics rights organisation. Enquiries concerning reproduction outside the scope of the above should be sent to the author of this book. You must not circulate this book in any other binding or cover and you must impose this same condition on any acquirer

Printed in the United States of America

©Adeola Babatunde 2013

info@adeolababatunde.com

ISBN 978-1-291-60860-1

Published by: David Daniel Consultancy Ltd

DO IT AFRAID

(Moving forward in the face of fear)

ADEOLA BABATUNDE

TABLE OF CONTENTS

Introduction	5
Strategy for Life Success	7
How to fight self – Limiting Beliefs	18
Think your way to Success	29
Worry Destroys Efficiency	40
Turning your problems into opportunities	49
You are not a Failure	59
You are who you think you are	72
Notes	81

INTRODUCTION

The sweetest victory is the one that's most difficult. The one that requires you to reach down deep inside, to fight with everything you've got, to be willing to leave everything out there on the battlefield — without knowing, until that do-or-die moment, if your heroic effort will be enough.

Society doesn't reward defeat, and you won't find many failures documented in history books. The exceptions are those failures that become stepping-stones to later success. Such is the case with Thomas Edison, whose most memorable invention was the light bulb, which purportedly took him 1,000 tries before he developed a successful prototype. "How did it feel to fail 1,000 times?" a reporter asked. "I didn't fail 1,000 times," Edison responded. "The light bulb was an invention with 1,000 steps."

Unlike Edison, many of us avoid the prospect of failure. In fact, we're so focused on not failing that we don't aim for success, settling instead for a life of mediocrity. When we do make missteps, we gloss over them, selectively editing out the miscalculations or mistakes in our life's résumé.

"Failure is not an option," NASA flight controller Jerry C. Bostick reportedly stated during the mission to bring the damaged Apollo 13 back to Earth,, and that phrase has been etched into the collective memory ever since.

For many in our success-driven society, failure isn't just considered an option—it's deemed a deficiency, says Kathryn Schulz, author of *Being Wrong: Adventures in the margin of Error".* *Of* all the things we are wrong about, this idea of error might well top the list," Schulz says. "It is our meta-mistake: We are wrong about what it means to be wrong. Far from being a sign of intellectual inferiority, the capacity to err is crucial to human cognition." The purpose of this book is to stir and challenge you.

CHAPTER 1

STRATEGY FOR LIFE SUCCESS.

Do you believe that there is a set of strategies that you can follow to achieve whatever you want in life? It's just like a formula. In this book, I will explain the simple strategies.

*Determine what you want to really achieve in Life:

This is the fundamental step in achieving what you want. You must first find out your destination before you make the move.

*Have a plan on how you can make your dream or goal come true:

You must develop your life plan which consists of your goals and your actual strategies of what you should do so that you will achieve your goals. Most people know what they want, but they never really have a clear plan on how they can achieve it. If you want to be successful, you must start from managing and planning for your future.

* Take consistent action that will get you to where you want to be:

Some people talk about what they want but they never really put it into action and actually make their dream come true. This is the biggest difference between a successful person and a person who is struggling. Successful people are committed to their dreams and goals. They are willing to do whatever it takes to achieve that which they have set out to achieve in life.

Let us consider this together, let's say I had a plan to go get groceries in a shop, to check my email when I get back and to work on my project proposal. Just about the time I am about to leave the house, let's say the

Phone starts ringing and I pick it up. It happens to be a childhood friend going through a situation. I am on the phone with him for a long time, and after our conversation, I realise that time has gone and there is no time for me to do all that I have planned to do. So, I decide to leave everything till the following day. What do you call that? Procrastination! This happens to people all the time. What you are supposed to do today you want to leave it till tomorrow. When tomorrow comes, you want to leave it till the next day. This situation happens to many people every day with different results. Some people have reasons and excuses while others are unreasonable with themselves and others.

Have you asked yourself this question? How is it that some people succeed when others are left behind figuring it out? Those people who are left behind lack the ability to move past their own excuses. In every situation, there are choices that can be made to further what you are up to in every area of life. When you are focused and have a plan, there are no excuses or reasons that will keep you from achieving that which you have set out to achieve.

A person who has no focus or plan is prone to excusing themselves and others for what has or has not happened. Lack of focus and plan equals excuses and reasons. Think about this, if you are reading this book, you are looking for a way to build an unreasonable life. Any person living an unreasonable life finds ways to make things happen regardless of the situation or circumstances in which they find themselves. The excuses that would have been used are no longer there. So, they decided to make it unreasonable. That's doing it afraid regardless of the circumstances or the situations they find themselves; they have decided that they need to do it anyway. Are you someone like that? The most successful people in your company, neighbourhood, city, state, country and in the world are unreasonable with themselves and others. And this is how they have become successful.

HOW YOU CAN HAVE AN UNREASONABLE LIFE

I will give you five ways by which you can build yourself into this unreasonable life:

- **Recognise It when fear is present:** Without this recognition, the fear will continue to keep you complacent and paralysed. Recognition is the first action to take in building success.
- **Distinguish what you are afraid of:** When fear is present, it is usually a response to something we are resisting. Are you resisting being embarrassed, made fun of, looking like you are not smart or something else?
- **Affirm yourself:** Create a picture or a statement that represents who you see yourself being in the situation or what you want from it.
- **Act in the face of the fear:** Now that you have created an affirming statement for yourself, proceed to take action. Soldiers learn to do it afraid. Take that same mind-set and apply it to whatever you do in life. You can have fear and still accomplish your goal. One good thing is that once you have accomplished it, you would have learned so much, and that confidence would have been built. And then, you will have the ability to continue.
- **Expand your thought:** Expanded thought is the result of taking an action consistent with what you want to have. When you take an action in the face of fear, you expand your thought about yourself,

your abilities; your thought about others and how they perceive you, and what is possible in your own life. Expansion is growth.

What are you willing to do to get what you really want in life?

It is a great question and it seems that the answer should be really simple. But it isn't. In fact, the best way to start figuring out what you are willing to do is by finding out what you are not ready to do. When we are faced with problem or probably when we are in pain, we tend to say we are ready to do anything. And by anything, I mean anything that will make the pain go away. But when the pain is no longer there, we now change the tone from we are ready to do anything to something else. What exactly are you ready to do for that pain which you are facing to go away, in order to have the life of your dream? Would you be ready to quit your job, would you be ready to get new friends, would you be ready to sell your house, would you be ready to invest your savings, would you be ready to eat differently, or change how you spend your spare time? So many people say yes, they can do this, they can do that, but in reality we are not ready to do most of these things. Just by going through these few possibilities, you probably realise that there are things in your life that you really don't want to change. But what if you knew that to have what you really want that was exactly what you had to do? Would you do it?

How about this question: Is the thing you don't want to change bringing you happiness now?

If it isn't, why wouldn't you want to change it? It is like that analogy of cat and dog. Our wants in life are insatiable. You have a dog, but you prefer a cat. When you have a cat, you want a dog. For you to be able to have a dog and have a cat, you have to work towards having both at once. We want everything good for ourselves but how do we go around having those things? Do you know for you to be able to have the dog you may have to get rid of the cat? And for you to be able to have the cat you have to get rid of the dog? I am not saying you should kill the dog or kill the cat. I am saying, do away with one. But are we ready to do that? Most people are not ready to do this. You are not ready to live your comfort zone to be able to achieve what you want in life. I will like to give an example of this.

Once upon a time, there was a woman called Sandra, even though she didn't have a sweet relationship with her husband, the last thing she wanted to do was end the relationship because she was in agony. But she turned herself inside out trying to make things work, pretending that if she just tried harder, somehow that cat was going to turn miraculously into a dog and she would be happy. It is an analogy. She was absolutely willing to do anything to be happy; anything to make that soul-tearing pain go away; She was willing to do anything to stop her pain except leaving the situation that was causing the problem. Can you imagine that? Do you know what is causing your problem? For you to be able to get rid of that which is causing your problem, you must be ready to make some changes.

How then can you change what is happening to you? You know your problem already. What you should be thinking of is the solution. Get rid of that which is causing you problem, so that you will be able to enjoy your life. But most people are not ready to do it. Think of a situation right now that's causing you pain or confusion and ask yourself these two questions:

What am I willing to do to get out of the pain?

What am I not ready to do?

A Long time ago, a frog was sitting on the bank of a river, a scorpion soon came by, and requested that the frog should ferry him across the river. The frog then required how he was supposed to do this; then the scorpion said that he would jump on to his back and then the frog can swim across the river. The frog thought for a while and he was not too happy with the thought. He asked the scorpion what if you sting me during the process. The scorpion laughed and said he is not going to do that because: if I sting you, which means both of us will perish inside the river. Quite convinced with the scorpion's words, the frog decided to ferry him across the river.

As they reached the middle of the river, the frog had a sharp pain and realised to his utter consternation that the scorpion had stung him. Puzzled and bemused by this behaviour, the frog asked the scorpion, why did you do that when you promised that you were not going to do it? The scorpion then strained his voice, I am sorry, I have no control over my character, it's my habit to strike whoever I see, and to me you are just a target. I just couldn't resist stinging you. The frog then retorted; see now what you have done, because of your inability to control your instincts. You have put my life also at peril. We are both going to perish now. After saying this, both the frog and the scorpion drowned in the river.

What is the moral of this story?

It can be very difficult to change your attitude and character. It's your thoughts which become your deeds and your deeds become your habits, and your habits shape your character. So always remember to gravitate towards your positive thoughts and feelings for it will greatly help you to reshape your character. What exactly is that thing you need to change for you to be able to achieve that which you want to achieve? You must be ready to part with that thing. I know it may be difficult, but you have to work around it. That thing is causing you pain but you are still living with it. For you to be able to enjoy that which you have set out to achieve, you have to use a strategy. Think about that which you can do that will replace that which is giving you pain, and that way, you would be able to get rid of that which is giving you pain. Are you ready to do that? Are you ready to leave your comfort zone and go into the world unknown? That is exactly what successful people do.

Many years ago, a jobless man applied for the position of an office boy at a very big firm. The human resources manager interviewed him, and then gave him a test, clean the floor, you are hired, he said. The human resources manager asked him for his email address, this young boy replied, I don't have an email. I am sorry sir, said the human resources manager; if you don't have an email, how do you intend to do this job? This job requires you to have an email address. Do you know how to use the internet? The young boy said no. the human resources manager was so angry, he asked the man to leave his office. There is no way you can be an office boy if you don't know how to use the internet.

This boy looked at himself, he deepened his hand into his pocket and he came out with Ten pounds. He didn't know what to do next. He had hoped that he was going to get this job and this job would have helped him. He then decided to go to the super market to buy a 10kg tomato crate. This boy sold the tomatoes in a door to door round. In less than two hours, he succeeded in doubling his capital. He repeated the same operation three times and returned home with sixty pounds. This man realised that he could do this to survive. The following day, he woke up early in the morning and did the same thing. Then, it became a regular routine. He would wake up in the morning, go to the supermarket, buy tomatoes and go around selling.

In no time, he was able to buy a van, and then a truck and he had fleet of delivery vehicles. Few years later, he became one of the biggest retailers in his community. Then, he decided to have a life insurance. He went to an insurance broker, and he chose a protection plan. When the conversation was concluded, the broker asked him for his email so that he could send him copies of the insurance policy. This man replied, I don't have an email. You don't have an email, and you have succeeded in building an empire? Imagine what you would have been if you had an email, the broker asked jokingly. This young man looked at him and smiled, well maybe an office boy. "Why did you say office boy, asked the broker?" The young man decided to tell the broker what led him into the business he was doing. He told him how he went for a job interview and he was refused the job because he didn't know how to use the internet, and didn't have an email address.

What is the moral of this story? You can turn your weakness into something that will help you in life. The fact that you don't know how to use the internet doesn't mean you can't still do something good with your life. Some people have been rejected or condemned that they can't do something, they allow the condemnation to affect them by leaving everything. They think they are a failure. Look at what happened to this man. This man left the office with ten pounds and thought to himself;" what am I going to do with my life?" This man decided to take a bold step. He committed the ten pounds into something which was able to turn him to a rich man. You can do the same thing.

I will like to share another story with you.

This is the story of a ten year old boy who decided to study judo despite the fact that he had lost his left arm in a devastating car accident. The boy began a lesson with an old Japanese judo master. The boy was doing well. So, he couldn't understand why after three months of training, the master taught him only one move. Trainer, the boy finally said; "shouldn't I be learning more moves?"" This is the only move you know, but this is the only move you will ever need to know," the trainer replied. Not quite understanding, but believing in the trainer, the boy kept on training.

Several months later, the trainer took the boy to his first tournament, surprising himself; the boy easily won his first two matches. The third match proved to be more difficult, but after sometime, his opponent became impatient and charged, the boy used his one move to win the match. Still amazed by his success, the boy was now in the finals. This time, his opponent was bigger, stronger and much more experienced than him. For a while, the boy

STRATEGY FOR LIFE SUCCESS

appeared to be over matched. Concerned that the boy might get hurt, the referee called the time out. He was about to stop the match when the trainer intervened; "No, the trainer insisted, let him continue". Soon after the match resumed, his opponent made a critical mistake, he dropped his guard. Instantly, the boy used his move to pin him. The boy had won the match and the tournament, and he was declared the champion.

On the way home, the boy and the trainer reviewed every move in each and every match. Then the boy summoned the courage to ask him what he had wanted to ask him; " Trainer, how did I win the tournament with only one move?" "You won for two reasons", the trainer answered; "first, you have almost mastered one of the most difficult moves in all of judo. And secondly, the only known defence for that move is for your opponent to grab your left arm."

What is the moral of the story? This boy's weakness was turned to his biggest strength. The judo master was able to discover this boy's weakness i.e. he had one arm and he taught him the strategy which will help him to be able to manoeuvre things with his one arm. And this boy, in return was able to use that strategy to become a champion. You have it in you as well. What is the thing that you think is your weakness; you can turn it around if you have the right strategy. You can change it around to your advantage.

Once upon a time, there was a water bearer who had two large pots. Each hung on each end of a pole which he carried across his neck. One of the pots had a crack in it while the other pot was perfect and always delivered the full portion of water at the end of a long walk from the stream to the master's house. The cracked pot arrived only half full. For a full two years, this went on daily, and the bearer delivered only one and a half pot full of water in his master's house. Of course, the perfect pot was proud of its accomplishment, perfect to the end for which it's made. But the poor cracked pot was ashamed of its own imperfection and miserable that it was only able to accomplish half of what it has been made to do.

STRATEGY FOR LIFE SUCCESS

After two years, the cracked pot perceived itself to be a failure. The pot spoke to the water bearer one day, by the stream;" I am ashamed of myself, and I want to apologise to you". The bearer looked at the pot and said, "Why are you ashamed of yourself?" The pot said, "I have not been able to help you. I have been delivering half full all the time for two good years." Then the bearer looked at the pot and said;" I want you to do something for me as we go back to my master's house. Tell me what you see on your path of the road." On the way home, the cracked pot looked at its path and what the cracked pot saw were beautiful flowers. When they got home, the bearer then asked the cracked pot to tell him what it saw on its path of the way when they were coming home. And the cracked pot said it only saw beautiful flowers. The pot asked the water bearer how the flowers got there. "you are the one that did it". And the cracked pot said, " how?" The bearer then said, "I saw your flaw that you leak water all the time. I strategized by planting flowers on your path of the way. And you have watered these flowers for two years. Without you I wouldn't have been able to have lovely flowers for my master's garden."

Don't look at flaws in people's life; you can turn the flaws to your advantage. That is a very strong strategy. The key word for the strategy of success is this; **deadline**. You must have a deadline for everything you are doing. One thing is for you to have a goal; you know what you want to do, you have the master plan. But if you don't have a deadline, you will not be able to accomplish your mission on time. That is if you are able to accomplish it.

I will like to share with you, some of the strategies for life success. When your mind is pressured to produce fruitful result within a limited amount of time, your body reacts by taking a set course of action to achieve it at the giving time line. If you don't have deadlines you will be easily side tracked and eventually lose focus. But because of the deadline, you need to do things and you need to do them now. That is the strategy for life success.

How do you create a deadline and device your game plan?

- Think of a concrete goal.
- Set a deadline.
- Device your strategy for success.
- Record your experiences and monitor your progress.

Keep yourself from getting side tracked by constantly reminding yourself of your goals. Remember that each little thing you do right now will matter and will take you closer to achieving your goal.

CHAPTER 2

HOW TO FIGHT SELF LIMITING BELIEFS

Did you ever find yourself in a situation where you saw someone just becoming successful or achieve a certain breakthrough and you thought to yourself: "I can never do that"? Most of us probably have. This is the result of something called, self-limiting beliefs that have been rooted in your mind.

What are self-limiting beliefs?

Self-limiting beliefs are mental blocks, negative thoughts, psychological hindrances or inner monsters stored in your mind. They tend to have a negative effect on you and they greatly limit your ability and programme your mind to discard all possibilities of ever achieving your goals and ultimately your success.

There are numerous definitions of self-limiting beliefs, but in this book, I will touch on the six top ones that I personally feel, have the worst effect on people.

Let's explore them together:

* **Believing that you are not good enough to achieve anything**: This probably starts from the fact that you first thought that you are not smart enough, have no special abilities or qualities. And since you don't have them, then you are not worthy or you can't achieve anything great.

* **Believing that people don't generally like you**: Before I tackle this, I need you to understand that I am explaining this in terms of normal, natured and perhaps even a well-mannered person. And not in terms of a rude, insensitive or bad mannered person who deserves to be hated by people. This belief leads you to think that no one likes you or wants to be your friend because of your flaw or flaws. You generally accept that you will never be liked, hence stamped the belief in your mind.

* **Believing that you will be rejected:** This is a very common self-limiting belief which exists in many different types of individuals from different walks of life. It exists in a student who is fearful of asking a teacher for assistance, a worker asking a colleague for help and even children asking their parents for certain things because they don't want to be refused.

* **Believing that certain tasks are impossible to achieve:** It's prudent to know here that, I am not talking about universally or psychologically impossible tasks to achieve, such as; humans flying, a child being older than her parents or a fan being on and off at the same time. Rather, the tasks I am focusing on are those that have been proven time and time again to be very possible to be achieved. Yet, people with this belief, limit themselves by saying they simply cannot achieve these tasks because they lack the qualities, knowledge, tools, resources and so on.

* **Having one side track belief:** People with this thought believe that there is one solution to a particular equation, or simply put, there is only one way to perform a certain task or to do things. After trying the only way they know and it doesn't work for them, they will back out. They don't want to explore. They don't want an alternative. They don't have a plan B. They are just one sided.

* **Believing that you are destined for failure:** It will surprise you to know that there are people like that around. This is one of the most damaging self-limiting beliefs anyone can possess. Sadly, it exists in a huge percentage among us. People with this belief deeply believe that whatever they do, they will end up in failure. And because of this, they don't set out to try anything beneficial or they stop half way when they are faced with circumstances or situations. Limiting beliefs are usually formed in the very early stages of life. It starts when you are exposed to a new situation or new environment and

HOW TO FIGHT SELF LIMITING BELIEFS

your first experience in that situation is negative or unpleasant. If it were a one off occurrence, then it will not form your limiting belief. However, if you keep experiencing negative and unpleasant results in the same situation and environment, then you are going to start doubting yourself. You're going to start wondering if others are doing the right thing and what you are doing is wrong. As time goes on and you experience more negative results, the frequency which is increased by the doubts you already have, your doubt starts to grow stronger and stronger until it reaches the point where it becomes rock- solid belief that would have become deeply rooted in your mind. It has become part of your identity.

At this point, it's basically like you have no free will; you are a slave to your confrontation. It's going to take time and repetition of you proving your limiting beliefs wrong. The more you prove your limiting belief wrong, the weaker it becomes, until it eventually fades away and has no power over you anymore. The bonus is that, once your limiting belief starts to lose its power over you, you will become much more confident too. This way, the reinforcing circle becomes a positive one. Then your actions boost your confidence, which in turn boosts your result, which boosts your confidence even more, so take them out.

Many times over the years, I have heard a story about how the circle is used to train elephants. I sincerely hope that this practice is historical. The story goes that when a baby elephant was brought into the circle, it was immediately chained to a stick in the ground. As a youngster, the animal is conditioned to only move the distance allowed by the chain. As an enormous strong intelligent adult, the chain is replaced by a rope but the elephant still only moves the distance allowed by the rope because she thinks she is still held back by that strong heavy chain. The adult elephant could easily break the rope and stroll away from her confine, but she doesn't. She is controlled by her conditioning. Oh yes! The chain is now in her mind not on her leg. I encourage you to consider what chains are in your mind causing you not to change your life. This is the key to change, to break free of outdated, untrue and harmful beliefs. The elephant still saw a chain around her ankle, though it was only a rope, a rope she could easily break loose.

What ropes are you seeing in your life as a chain? Are you ready to stretch that rope or maybe, even break it?

Once upon a time, there was a woman whose son had a drug addiction problem. At significant personal financial expense, this woman actually kept a lawyer on retainer because he was always in court for drug related offences. She made excuses to his teachers and later his boss. It was a great inconvenience to her life. She drove him to and from work when he lost his driving licence. She allowed his family into her home, when they were evicted and didn't have anywhere to stay. When this man started stealing her money, she could not tell anybody.

To most of us reading this story, this woman's rope is pretty obvious, "cut it loose", you are probably yelling by now. This woman's perspective was different. In her mind, she didn't see her 27 years old son as an adult. She still saw a frightened, hurting, angry little boy. After several years, and thanks to counselling, coaching and supporting group of parents like her. This woman chose to change how she looked at her son's situation. When she changed, it changed. When she tends to test the strength of the rope of her behaviour which placed her son's needs above her own, she empowered herself and empowered her son to begin taking responsibility for his own life. Eventually, she stopped driving him, so he took the bus to work and he arrived on time. She gave him thirty days to move out of her home, and in that time frame, he found a small apartment for his family. When he was on his own, his mum wasn't constantly checking up on him, telling him to get help. He also sought counsel for his addictive habit. When this woman chose to break free from the old pattern of making everything okay for her son, things became much more okay for her. When she changed the way she looked at things, that is, when she let go of the belief that she was responsible for making her son's life work for him, the things she looked at, changed. She saw that he was an adult making poor choices, partially reinforced by the enabling behaviours. This woman's early behaviour was a chain of outdated beliefs and misplaced guilt.

When she saw that the chain was really a breakable rope, she began to test its strength much to her satisfaction. Her son is now taking responsibility for his life. When you change the way you look at things, the things you look at change. Like this woman, each of us see chains where there are only breakable ropes. I encourage you today to look at that which is stopping you from achieving that which you want to achieve and break loose.

What is the moral of this woman's story?

Human beings are subject to self-limiting beliefs especially during childhood, when most of us genuinely, physically, mentally and emotionally incompetent, knew otherwise. We look up to the adults for emulation and guidance. When limitations are imposed, we tend to view it as a permanent part of our identity. Not realizing that we can overcome limitations. Especially with the proper mind-set, thinking, training and experience.

Change your thought, change your belief, identify what has been holding you back, and challenge them. Hold on to the fact that the belief can be overcome. Break through this limiting belief and change your performance, change your result and change your life. You can do it.

Once upon a time, there was a little dog that was always chained to a tree for several years when outside of the house. The chain was twenty feet, and the dog would run as far as that

HOW TO FIGHT SELF LIMITING BELIEFS

twenty feet and stop. This went on for so many years. Finally, the owner of the dog felt sorry for it and removed the chain. The dog would still run twenty feet and stop, even the cat that tormented it for so many years by staying just a few feet away from the chain was safe. The dog will run to the twenty foot mark and just short of the cat and stop, no longer held back by the chain but by the conditioning of its own limiting beliefs. A couple more steps and the dog could have walked through it forever. Just a couple more steps, and so can you. That is the good and exonerating news; we can identify and let go of our limiting beliefs. Are you ready to do that? What is holding you back? Stop seeing the chain. Look at the rope which you can break loose.

Two years ago, I happened to meet a woman at the supermarket who wanted to pursue her life dream of having her own business. She worked for a Group Home as a day provider but wanted to establish a better control of her destiny. She was hesitant to do this. Afraid that she wouldn't be able to make enough money to quit her boring day job, her biggest challenge to succeed was not her ability. It was her belief in herself. This woman had a self-limiting belief. Most of her friends and her acquaintances doubted her ability to be a business owner. They advised her to keep doing that job which was giving her pain. At least, she was able to get some money to pay her rent and look after her daily needs. Fortunately for this woman, she didn't want to totally give up her idea. while she continued to have a nagging doubt about what she wanted to do, her goal was totally supported by a new business acquaintance. Her business acquaintance gave her encouragement, made time available whenever she needed questions or suggestions, or just to talk about business issues.

Although, she had the right plan and ability to succeed, she remained her own worst obstacle. The good news is that she continued even though she struggled with self-doubts, but persevered and quit her day job eventually. What she conquered was much more than issues around developing her business. She conquered her own apprehension, her own self-

doubt. She succeeded because she didn't listen to the naysayers. She succeeded because she overcame the greatest obstacle, her unbelief in herself.

How do you see yourself?

You have a dream. You want to go out and do something, but you are so scared to leave your comfort zone. This happens to so many people. Because something is happening to you, you love it where you are. You don't want to step out into the world unknown. Successful people take risks. You must be ready to step into the world unknown for you to be able to achieve that which you want to achieve.

This woman in the story actually wanted something good for herself. She wanted to have her own business. But she was filled with her self- limiting beliefs, scared that she wouldn't be able to handle it. Those she turned to for advice discouraged her . Instead of lifting her up, they said things which would make her remain where she was. They said: "Stay where you are and continue to make your little money". You have people like that around you.

You can't blame anybody for who you are today. You are hundred per cent responsible for the actions you take. You can't blame your Father; you can't blame your Mum. You can't blame your Friends. Yes, they advised you. So what? So many people will advise you. It is your responsibility to check out which one is in line with your dream. Stop limiting yourself. This woman was bored doing that which she was doing. She wanted to fulfil her destiny of having her own business. Yet, she didn't have what it takes. She limited herself by thinking that she would not be able to handle it.

HOW TO FIGHT SELF LIMITING BELIEFS

Who do you think you are?

How do you see yourself? What exactly is that thing you want to do and accomplish? What is that negative thing telling you? You can change your negative thoughts around to something positive. That is the only way you can get that which you want from life. We all have this subconscious mind that comes in when we are thinking of something positive. Especially, when you want to do something that will make you successful. Your subconscious mind will start telling you, "You can't do it. "You don't have what it takes. You don't have the financial resources. You don't have the tools". You have to change your reasoning from that to something positive. Look out for people who have been able to do it without anything. Look at how they were able to do it and emulate that. Learn how they did it.

You want to go for a job? You are already thinking you are too short or probably you are too tall for the job. You have already bombarded yourself with such negative thoughts. Do you think you will be able to get something positive from the interview? You have to change your reasoning. Change your mind-set. Work positively towards achieving that which you are looking for in life. Stop limiting yourself. Let's say you wanted to go and win a race; by the time you got there, because they said the person next to you had won the race four times before, you looked at yourself and said, "Why bother, that person is going to win again". Do you think with that self-limiting belief, you will be able to win? Of course, you won't be able to win. You have to change that self-limiting belief into something positive.

How do you remove your self-limiting beliefs?

- Identify the fact that you have it in you. You need to know exactly what thoughts and beliefs you have that have stopped you from being happy and from reaching your goals. For example, are you happy with your present financial situation? If not, then, why not? Is it because you believe it's hard to make money? Is it because you believe that you are not smart enough to have your own business? Is it because you believe you can't get a better job? All of these I have mentioned are limiting beliefs.

- Once you have identified your limiting beliefs; in all areas of your life: business, dating, social, health and so on, then you can start working on how to remove them. I can't stress enough how important it is to observe yourself and try to identify your limiting beliefs. Everyone has at least one, but some people have dozens. I used to have so many limiting beliefs. And I have slowly walked my way through them. I still have limiting beliefs today, and whenever I discover one, I immediately work on removing it.

- Personally, I found that the best way to remove a limiting belief is to prove that it's irrational and fake. You do this with corporate proofs and logical evidence. Find examples of people who have achieved what your limiting belief is telling you is not possible. If you think you are poor because you are dump and don't have a degree, then make it your mission to find three or more people without a degree who are making a lot of money. If you are massively overweight and you think it's impossible to get into shape, and become healthy, find three or more people who used to be overweight and managed to *get slim*. By doing this, you prove to yourself that your limiting belief is exactly what you think it is. Now, you can say to yourself, "If They can do it, so can I". Think about this.

Keep in mind that you can do whatever you set out to do, what you just need to do is to work positively towards doing it. If they could do it, you as well can do it. Who says you cannot be a good actor? Who says you cannot be a good singer? Who says you cannot own your own business? You can do all these things by changing your mind-set from something negative to something positive.

What is holding you back?

Stop focusing on those who were not able to do it. Those people decided to quit because they didn't have a dream. Look out for successful people who have been able to do that thing and they did it successfully.

That you have done it once or a few times, and you didn't get it right doesn't make you a failure. You will only be a failure if you quit. For you to be able to achieve that which you are looking for, step out of that self-limiting belief today and work towards getting what you want for yourself. That relationship is not making you happy, but you are so scared. You are thinking; "let me continue to cope". "It will get better". He comes back home every night, beats you up, does all sorts of things to you, and abuses you. Instead of you taking the bold step, you limit yourself by thinking if I tell him I am not happy with what he's doing; all he's going to do is to beat me again. Why not take that bold step and let him know that you are not happy with what he's doing, 'Never say Never'. That may change him. I don't know whether you realise that most people complain to the wrong people. You are at work, they have done something wrong to you, instead of telling the person who has done that wrong thing, for that person to be able to change what he or she has done, you will not tell them. You will go home and talk about what has happened at work. You will then go back to work and tell the people what has happened to you at home. Why not face the people so that they can change that which they have done. You have to be ready to take a bold step. Stop limiting yourself.

Well, it's not a bad thing to say that you want to be conscious. But it's better to be conscious than to be scared. When you are scared of doing something, you will never achieve it. You must be ready to step out of your self-limiting beliefs. Stop seeing yourself as somebody who cannot do it. Work on it positively and you will get it.

You see somebody with something good, Oh yes! You appreciate what they have got, but you assume that they can never be for you. You know that job you are doing is not good for you. You can't look after your children. It doesn't even give you time to be with your family. You know you have a dream of having your own business; you are limiting yourself because you have assumed that if you leave that job, you won't be able to cope. You have to stop limiting yourself. Take the bold step and work positively towards getting your own thing. You can do it. If those successful people could do it, you can do it as well.

CHAPTER 3

THINK YOUR WAY TO SUCCESS

You may be surprised to learn that being successful is no more difficult than being a failure. It's just different and the key is in your thinking.

According to Tony Robins, 80% of the road to success is in the way you think. While 20% is in the actions you take. I am sure, you are thinking," Could this be really true". Well, it's pretty simple. Your life is a reflection of what you think most of the time. Let's say your prevailing thoughts were that life is difficult and you are unlikely to get anywhere. Do you think with your head full of those thoughts, you will be able to recognise the greatest opportunity imaginable even if it is right in front of you? Probably not.

Most times, we tell people we had a dream. You know what you want to do. You have a passion for something. But all you would do is to talk about it. Why not put in the 20% which is required by taking action. If you don't take action, you won't be able to achieve what you want to achieve. Imagine you had 80% to think about your dream, to work out how you are going to make it a reality. But, you don't put in the 20% which is required by taking ACTION, that's what Tony is talking about. The 20% is what most people don't have. They don't ACT.

I will like to share a story with you. This is about a boy from a very poor Family. The Father happened to be the breadwinner of the Family, and not that he had a good job. He was a gardener. He goes around helping people to look after their gardens. Sometimes, people don't even pay him on time. His Mum happened to be disabled. This boy was constantly absent from school for lack of money to buy books, school uniform and shoes. His friends didn't make it easy for him as well. Can you imagine, let's say your name is Paul, Simon, Solomon but your friends looked at your situation and now gave you a nickname. Do you know what they called this boy? Poverty! Imagine being called poverty because of your situation. It was that bad for this boy. At first, he reported his friends to his teachers, they got disciplined for this. They still didn't stop. Any time they had the opportunity of calling him poverty, they would still call him poverty.

One day, after being absent from school for a long time, he went to school and he saw a friend of his. His friend said, "Poverty, what happened to you, we have not seen you for a few days now?" Just when he was about to tell his friend what happened, two other friends joined them and they all said, "Poverty, what is going on, you have not been around for a while now?" Then this young boy looked at them and said "well, some people were meant to pay my Dad but they didn't pay him and because there was no money to bring to school, I couldn't come to school". Just about the time they were talking, a car drove past them and one of them said, "Wow!, nice car. When I grow up I will like to have such car". They all acknowledged that it was a good car.

Then, they started talking about who they wanted to be in the future. One of them said he would like to be a lawyer, another one said a doctor, the third person said an engineer. The three of them looked on, waiting for this boy called Poverty to say who he would like to be in the future. As though he knew what they were thinking, he didn't say anything. Then, one of them asked him, "Poverty, what about you?" Poverty said "well, do you want to know my ambition? My ambition is to be a successful businessman."

The three of them looked at him and laughed. One of them said, "You! Businessman? Do you know what it takes to be a businessman? You can't even afford to buy textbooks. Don't you know you have to go through college and university before you can be successful, how do you intend to achieve that?" This young boy called Poverty, looked at them and said; "well, that's your opinion. Keep your opinion about me and let me keep my ambition". What do you call that? Positive reasoning and determination.

This young boy refused to be condemned by his friends. He asked them to keep their opinion about him and then he would keep his own ambition. How do you see yourself? You have people around you who will run you down because of your situation. They will *look at you and say you can't achieve that which you had set out to achieve. If you allow them to condemn you, then, it will affect you. It's one thing for them to say things about you, but another thing for you to take what they say on board. This young boy, full of determination, said to his friends," keep your opinion about me, I will keep my own ambition".*

Few months later, the Father of this young boy became sick. Don't forget I said he is the bread winner of the Family. Which means, it will switch from the man to this young boy now? The young boy had to stop going to school so that he could look for a job and look after the Family. After walking around for a long time, he was able to get a job at a car wash. He started helping them to wash cars. From the money he made, he was able to look after the Family. After a while, he started saving some money. With the money he made from the car wash he was able to see himself through Secondary School, college and University. After graduation, he had his own little business. In no time, he became rich. Some of his friends, who were there when he said he was going to be a successful business man, even came to his company to see him. They were surprised. "Determination" is the word.

In life you are going to be faced with situations, circumstances, obstacles, especially as you work your way through success. The way you handle your situation will determine the outcome you are going to get. Some people find it so difficult to live with situations. Look at this boy's situation, the Father who was the bread winner of the Family became sick. This means, there was no money to send him to school. Because of this boy's determination, he took the bull by the horn. He decided to take charge. He started looking after the family with the money he made from the car wash; he was able to see himself through school. You can do the same thing.

I will like to share another story with you. This story is about me. Oh yes! When I was young, I had a dream of becoming a lawyer. You know we all have dreams. Some people want to become engineers, some want to be accountants; some people want to be medical doctors. My own dream was to be a lawyer, and I worked positively towards achieving my dream. As I was going through this, I had a situation along the way, but let's leave that for later. I got to secondary school. In my final year of secondary school, I had to sit for the exam to go to university. The form given to me then had two choices. So, in my first choice I picked Law and I picked Dramatic Arts for my second choice. Not that I wanted to study dramatic Arts. I just picked it because there was no other course I could pick at that time. When I sat for the exam, unfortunately, my score wasn't up to that of Law. So, I settled for my second choice which was Dramatic Arts. I said to myself that in my second year of studying Dramatic Arts I was going to change my course to Law. But when I started studying Dramatic Arts, I fell in love with it. So, I graduated studying Dramatic Arts.

After graduation, I had my own little business, and then I settled down. (I got married and had children). One day I was in the office, there was need for me to prepare a letter to present in Court, I tried my best possible, but the letter wasn't just good enough. I made a call to a friend of mine who was a lawyer at that time. This man came to my office and we sat down. He looked at the letter for me and said, "Well for me to be able to rewrite this letter properly for you, you will have to pay me". I said, "You are my friend. Why do you want me to pay for just a letter of few lines?" You will not believe it. He refused to write the letter for me until I gave him the money he had requested for. He wrote the letter for me and he left.

I sat down after he had left and said to myself, "Do you know you wouldn't have paid anything for this letter if only you have been able to pursue your dream of studying Law?" I picked the phone and called few universities.

There was no luck for the first one week of calling. Eventually, after calling severally, I was invited into one of the Universities for interview and I was given admission to study Law.

I will tell you one thing. When people tell you that they had to leave their comfort zone to make their dream a reality, don't doubt them. Imagine someone who has a family, a business to run and then decided to go into the university to study Law. That person was me. The road to success is not usually so easy. You will be faced with situations, you may have to let go of certain things for you to be able to achieve it. In my situation, I was able to joggle things around even though it was tough. At the end of the day, I was able to achieve my dream of becoming a lawyer.

Don't forget I said earlier I had situations, as I was thinking about my way to being a lawyer. My circumstance was when I was in secondary school. My mathematics teacher made it so difficult for all of us in the class. This man would come to the classroom and stand by the door, when you say, "Good morning Sir", the first thing he's going to say in response is " two times two times four plus eight plus nine plus eleven plus all that". This man would make it so difficult for you to even be able to calculate. Before you say, "Em". He would say, well, you, you, you, and ask all the people he had pointed at, to come out. Do you know what this man would do? He would start beating us; he would beat us to the extent that it will be so difficult for us to be able to understand that which he's there to teach us. This went on for so long.

Then one day, I said to myself," if I continue like this, I will not be able to achieve my dream of becoming a lawyer". Because that time, for you to be able to study Law, you will need to pass mathematics and English. If you pass all other subjects and you fail mathematics and English, you cannot study Law. Then I thought about what I could do, I got home one day, and then I told my Mum about my situation, "Mum I have a problem. There is this mathematics teacher who is always coming to the classroom to beat us". My Mum requested to see the Principal of the School and told him all that I said. The Mathematics teacher was also invited by the Principal. It turned out that I was not the first student to tell my parent about him. The principal said he was going to look into it. Few days later, I was invited into the office of the Principal, and asked by the principal to go to another class. But for the fact that I refused to suffer in silence, I wouldn't have been able to learn Mathematics.

I'm not saying you should go around reporting your teachers to your parents. What I am saying is, you know what you are looking for and you know how to get what you are looking for. If you see that something will affect or disturb what you are looking for in life, work your way around it. My own obstacle was that Mathematics teacher who was always beating us. I wasn't good at Mathematics then. I gave it everything because I wanted to pass the subject. It was like he was only coming to the classroom because of me. That was the way I saw it then. You can change your situation around by speaking up. There is no harm in you saying this is what you are going through. Talk to people and let them help you out.

I will like to give you another example; this is about a friend of mine when we were young. His name is mark. He wanted to be a footballer. We got to secondary school, he played for the school. He represented us in so many Matches. One day, we went for a match, and on the field of play, somebody slumped next to Mark and died. This really affected Mark. He said he wasn't going to play football anymore. I talked to him, he didn't listen to me. Some other friends talked to him as well. He still refused. Then, we went to our sport teacher, and this man was able to convince him. Then he started playing for us again. As we speak, this man is now a very rich man. He retired as a professional footballer years back. He was able to bounce back from his situation. So many people find it difficult to bounce back. Mark's situation was the person who slumped next to him and died.

How do you handle circumstances? How do you handle your problem? You know who you want to be, you know what you want for yourself in life. But, when you're faced with situations, how do you handle it?

In life, for you to be able to achieve what you want to achieve, you must think like a baby and act like a baby. Oh yes! I will tell you what I am talking about. You know, babies can't talk. So, what they do is to use what they have got to make you know that which they want. They will cry. They will cry so very much until you check out to see what's happening to them that is making them uncomfortable. They make it so difficult for you to be able to do anything by crying. That's what I call, "taking action". So, for you to be able to achieve what you want to achieve, you must act like a baby. That is, work positively towards what you want to achieve in life. It is not enough for you to have 80% to think and not use the 20% to take action. That's what Tony Robins said. We use 80% to think of what we want to do, we plan what we want to do. But if you don't take the 20% action required, you won't be able to achieve what you want to achieve. You can do it. All it will take is for you to stop procrastinating. Stop thinking that you will do it tomorrow, and when tomorrow comes, you say, you will do it tomorrow. People like this don't get things done. The way to get it done is for you to do it today. Think of what you want to do and work positively towards achieving it today. There is no harm in you asking people to help you out. You have people around you. Some will lift you up, while some will bring you down. If you discuss your vision with people and they say to you, "you can't do it". Don't be angry with them. Just walk away from such people. I call them dream stealers. They don't share your vision. Look for people that will lift you up by telling you, "You can do it". The fact that your friends have said you cannot do something doesn't mean that you cannot do it. You have to be ready to face your situations. You are hundred percent responsible for the actions you take in Life. You are who you are today because of the actions you have taken or the ones you have refused to take.

Keys to think your way to Success.

* Think for yourself: There is no harm with you discussing your situations with people or telling them about your vision. But you have to be ready to take the required action yourself.

* Have clear goals in mind: You must be specific. You must have a clear goal in mind. Know that which you want for yourself. You want to be a lawyer, work positively towards what you want to achieve. Don't say, "Oh, I want to be a lawyer, but if I can't get that one, maybe I should be a doctor or probably an engineer". People like that are called jack of all trades, master of none.

* Don't Wait for Opportunities, Create One: Some people say that they want to wait for opportunities to come. If you want to wait for an opportunity to come before you take action, you may not be able to achieve anything in life. If you're serious about creating lasting and significant things in your world, you must take action, as opposed to you just thinking without taking action.

Strategies to think your way to Success

- **Know what success is:** If you don't know what success is for you, how can you probably create it. Success is a different thing for different people. One person's success may be another person's catastrophe. That's because success is not so much about the situation, circumstances, events or outcomes, as it is about what that thing means to that person in the middle of it. In order to create success, you must first define it, and far too many people haven't. Be very clear about what you want and how you want to achieve it in life. Clarity produces excitement, excitement produces momentum, momentum produces behavioural change, behavioural change produces a different result and eventually, the internal vision becomes an external reality.
- **Get comfortable being uncomfortable:** Oh yes, some people will live a life of second best, of compromise and under-achievement simply because they are controlled by fear. People who always take the easy option are destined for mediocrity. You have to learn to leave your comfort zone and move into the world unknown. That's what successful people do.
- **Seek to be righteous, not right:** The need to be right speaks of all arrogance, insecurity, ego and stupidity. It's also synonymous with failure. The person who constantly needs to be right will miss out on much of what life has to teach him and annihilate him from others. Arrogance repulses, humility attracts.
- **Seek respect and not popularity**: It's been said that our nature is who we are and our reputation is who people think we are. When the two are synonymous, we're usually on the right path.

- **Embrace mess:** To embrace mess is to embrace life because life is 'messy', unpredictable, unfair, uncertain, lumpy, and bumpy. So get used to a little chaos in life, embrace it even.

- **Don't become your parents, your boss or anyone, but you:** Don't get me wrong, I am not saying that you should not respect your parents, by all means respect them. Respect your boss, respect elders, but what I am saying is, don't become them. You are who you think you are. Think for yourself. Think about who you want to be and work positively towards being who you want to be.

- **Use more of what you already have:** Imagine what you could achieve if you took all the knowledge, intelligence, opportunities, time, skills and the talents that you currently have and absolutely milk it? What if you already have more than enough talent to become successful? Well, you do and there goes the excuses and that voice that is telling you right now that you don't have what it takes to become successful; that is called fear not logic, fear not reality, fear, unless of course you allow that to become your reality. Be mindful that the voice in your head, the very loud, annoying and persistent one is really a reflection of your potential and mostly a manifestation of your insecurity. And now, you are not alone in your self-doubt. It's a universal condition. Many people fail, not because they don't have what it takes but because they don't know how to go about it. Successful people typically don't have much more innate potential, luck, time or opportunity than the next person, but they consistently find the way to use much of what they have at their disposal.

- **Be an innovator and not an imitator**: You know what you want for yourself. You want to be a doctor, but your friend is a lawyer. You have friends who are accountants. You have friends who are engineers. Don't imitate them.

- **Do what most people won't do**: If you want to achieve what most people won't achieve, such as: happiness, joy, calm, wealth, optimal health and balance, then don't do what they do. If you want to be like the majority, then do what they do. Producing different result comes from doing something that is so different from other people. Most people won't persevere. They won't finish what they have started. They won't do what it takes. They won't be solution focused. They won't do what scares them and won't be the change they want to see in the World. Choose to be different and that's the only way you can do it.

CHAPTER 4

WORRY DESTROYS EFFICIENCY

What do you understand by fear?

Is there any major difference between fear and being afraid? Well! Fear is an unpleasant and often strong emotion caused by anticipation or awareness of danger. Fear is completely natural and it helps people to recognise and respond to dangerous situations and threat. While being afraid, indicates a state of action symbolic of the fright or fight concept.

What am I talking about? If you are afraid, you have the ability to act. That is, you decide whether or not you will stay and deal with the perceived threat. Whereas, if you have fear, you simply have a condition from which no action may arise. This implies that fear is paralysing, disabling the ability to act because there is nothing specific from which action may come about. Fear is a stealer of human potential.

Once upon a time, there were two friends. One named Paul, the other one David. Paul is a timid person while David is a goal-getter. These two friends after college decided to set up a security company. They went for necessary security training. And after their training, they wrote proposals which they sent out to different companies requesting to provide security services for them. After trying severally, they were able to start running a company for somebody.

A Few months later, one man walked up to them to say he's got a company and he would like these two friends to provide security services for him as well. Paul, being a timid guy, was quick to tell this man, "sorry our hands are full, we can't do it". But David looked at Paul and said, "What is going on, why did you say we cannot do it? We have always talked about expanding. Don't you know this is an opportunity for us to expand?" David told Paul that they were going to do it. But Paul still went on to say: "Don't you know we are going to fail if we try? Having another company to run is going to be a task for us. We are going to need more hands. I can hardly manage myself let alone manage other people."

You have always been talking about opportunities. Most people don't even know when they see an opportunity. These two friends saw an opportunity. And instead of Paul to appreciate this opportunity and work positively towards making this happen, he decided that he was so comfortable where he was. Is that who you are? You are scared to leave your comfort zone and go into the world unknown. How then do you want to achieve that which you want to achieve in life? David insisted that they should take the job, and they were able to run this company for that man successfully. As we speak today, these two friends have got a big company. But for David, they wouldn't have been able to achieve what they have achieved today.

In life, you must learn to do it afraid. That is the difference between successful people and those who are not able to make it. When successful people see a situation like that, they see it as a great opportunity and they work positively towards achieving that which they want to get out of it. You can do the same thing. If you are waiting for your opportunity to come, there is no way you will know when opportunity comes. You have to do it while you are still afraid. That is the only way out. You are not ready to leave your comfort zone because you are so happy with your 9 a.m. to 5 p.m. job. Even though you had a dream, you are scared that if you stop your 9 a.m. to 5 p.m. job, you won't be able to get to where you want to get to in life. You are scared to pursue your dream because you are not sure of what will happen should you decide to pursue it. You will remain where you are and continue to suffer in silence. That's the way it is in life.

Some people will say they want to wait for fear to go before they do what they want to do. If you want to wait, you are going to wait forever, because fear will remain there. Do you know how this happens? When you are thinking of something positive, you have this thing called your subconscious mind which will start telling you how difficult it will be, how you won't be able to achieve it, how people will ridicule you, how you are going to be a failure. If you are not able to fight this subconscious mind, which is telling you something negative, you will remain where you are.

You want to go for a job interview but you are scared that you are too short or probably you are too tall or you are thinking you don't have the experience required. If you bombard yourself with such negative thoughts, do you think you will be able to achieve what you want to achieve? You will get there and you will mess everything up. That is the way it is in life. Change that negative reasoning to something positive for you to be able to get what you want to get in life. What am I talking about? Do it afraid! Successful people do it while they are scared. Be ready to leave your comfort zone for the world unknown. That is the only way to do it.

How can you fight your fear?

Fear is something we deal with every day. Some carry their own around. The most important tool in the fight against fear is to name it. While seemingly obvious and easy to do, this is a very difficult task and not to be taken lightly. One reason why it's so hard to name fear is that the human mind is very subtle and can trick its owner into thinking that fear has been named when only a superficial or symptomatic symbol of the fear has been identified. The second reason why it is so difficult for us to name our fear is that we invest heavily in our fear. It takes great effort to build fear and maintain it. Removing this fear brings the threat of internal judgment about the cause of that investment and its relative worth. So once again, a fear holder will tend to avoid naming it so that he or she does not have to face the reality of having invested in something of little or no value.

Fear is hard to fight because it has no face. No substance, it is the nameless unknown. The natural inclination of humankind is to resist the unknown. Fear is a sneaky thing which creeps up on us when we least expect it. It can cripple our souls and steal our dreams of being successful. If I told you all my silly fears, you would have laughed because the list goes on and on and on forever. But I have learnt that amazing thing. I do it afraid. I step outside of my comfort zone and I fight my fear. You can do the same thing.

Why is it so easy to let fear stand between us and our dreams? Do you know how it all works out?

First, we think of something that we really want to accomplish. Then we start to list all the great benefits that this venture will bring into our lives. And just when we are really getting into it, some part of our mind comes up with;" Oh, are you sure this one will work? Are you sure this is the right thing to do? People will ridicule you". Do you know what will follow? A list of negative possibilities designed to throw a wet blanket over our great idea. And what do you call this? We call it a reality check. But is that the accurate thing? No! Why do people repackage fear and call it reality? We do it because calling it reality makes hope and dream seem like fantasies and saves us from having to face our fear. Or put another way, we do it because we are afraid.

I will like to share another story with you. This is the story of a young boy called Daniel. After his master's degree in law, he decided to pursue his PhD. He wrote a proposal which he sent out to some universities. Eventually, he was invited by some of the

WORRY DESTROYS EFFICIENCY

universities he had sent proposals to. He picked the one he wanted and he went there. On getting to this particular university, there was a professor who was asked to interview him. The professor looked at this young man and said to him, having gone through your proposal; I want you to do something for us which will help to know whether we will give you admission. Daniel looked at this professor and said: "what do I have to do sir?" Then the professor said to him; "I want you to come and deliver a lecture". This young boy was surprised, "Lecture! Sir, I don't want to be a lecturer. I just want to study for my PhD". This professor looked at him and said "well, delivering a lecture will help to know whether you will be able to handle that which you want to do. Don't be scared. You are not going to be taking students. It's just going to be five Lecturers: I and four other lecturers. I will give you materials you can work with and the links you can use to do your research. If you want to do it, you will be expected to come back to this university in two weeks".

Daniel looked at this man. He wanted his PHD and he loved the university. He said he was going to do it. So, he was given reading materials with some links to use for his research. This young boy went home and he started preparing himself for this lecture. The very day he was meant to go for the lecture, something set in. Do you know what happened to him? Fear set in. You know when you are about doing something, especially as you are working on something, your subconscious mind will start telling you: "Do you think this will work? This is not for you. You are going to fail. Don't forget you are going to be facing professors and doctors, those who are much more intelligent and learned. How will you cope?" This young boy was able to fight his subconscious mind to stand still. He knew that, what was required for him to be able to achieve that which he has set out to achieve is to go and do it. He left his house, and when he got to the university, that professor was waiting for him.

The professor then took him to where another four professors were. When he got to this room, he was a bit scared. The professor said; "well, now we are here. What have you got for us?" Just about the time this young boy was about to start delivering his lecture, do you know what happened again? His Fear came back. This time he told himself that, if he does not do it, he won't be able to achieve his dream. This young boy did it afraid. He delivered the lecture and he did it really well. At the end, all the lecturers clapped for him. The professor shook hands with him. He was given admission. That way, he was able to study for his PhD in that university.

Daniel did it afraid. He didn't allow his subconscious mind to take over his life. One thing is for you to have a dream, if you do not pursue your dream by doing it afraid, you may not be able to achieve it. This young boy fought his subconscious mind which was telling him that those people were superior people. He was able to do that and I believe you can do the same thing. What is that thing you want to go in for? Your mind is telling you it will not work. It will work if you put in your best. It will work if you do it while fear is still there.

Why are we afraid?

The list will vary depending on the situation but some likely candidates are:

- Fear of the unknown
- Fear of risks
- Fear of failure
- Fear of ridicule
- Fear of change

Now, we only need one or two of these to dispense with minor aspirations. On the other hand, if we are trying to talk ourselves out of a major dream or goal, we may need to mobilise a small army of fear to get the job done. And how do we justify getting in on our own way like that? Once again, we call it reality. When we hide behind the term reality, it makes us reasonable instead of fearful. It's like saying that any other choice is just playing foolishly. And now we can retire back into the safety of our comfort zone without losing face. Our own sense of insecurity makes us feel protected inside that wall. So we find a reason to stay there out of harm's way.

The problem is, we also wall ourselves off from all the wonderful opportunities and its purity that makes life fun. Without risk, there is no sense of adventure, no excitement and no passion. Before I go any further, let's acknowledge that a manageable amount of conscious apprehension is not a bad thing. Rushing into something without taking the time to weigh the possible adverse consequences is not usually the course of wisdom. In fact, a manageable amount of fear can also be transmuted into excitement and motivation. So, the kind of fear we are concerned with, is the type that limits our ability and willingness to reach our dream. Any kind of fear that hinders our ability to act in the direction of our heartfelt desire is a serious handicap that needs to be addressed. The hidden reason why fear can move us to compromise our goals and abandon our dreams is the fact that insecurity is the granddaddy of all limiting emotions.

Every person on the planet has an inherent and an insatiable desire to feel safe and secure. On the subconscious emotional level, we would naturally try to avoid anything perceived as a threat to our sense of security. It is important to realise that most of these negative emotional anchors are only perception. They have little or nothing to do with any real threat. Then again, life is perception, so to us, they will be as real as we choose to see them. The key to breaking down these walls and evacuate the fear is found in our ability to alter the way we perceive any situation and the emotional anchor attached to it. We don't need to change reality; just our emotional interpretation of it. This is where learning a few adverse life skill gives us a total control of how we feel and how we experience life.

Have you ever wondered why some people embrace challenges that cause others to retire to safety? How can the same experience represent excitement to one person and paralysing fear to another? We may be tempted to attribute a difference to the place of self-confidence but where does self-confidence come from? Self-confidence is what results when our perception is reinforced by our experiences. The thing to keep in mind is that our perception has a strong influence on our level of commitment which often determines whether or not we succeed in life. How much difference can you create with such a little shift in perception?

Sometimes, the difference between a happy and successful outcome and failure is only a slight shift in perception. How we represent things to ourselves determines how we will respond to any given situation. In turn our response will help to determine the outcome. When life hands you a challenge, how do you feel about it? What is your initial internal response to an emotional situation? What is your external response as seen through your body language and verbal expressions? Why does it even matter? Changing the way we deal with impending danger or tragedy is much evolved. These are either major emotional events which involved the healing process or sudden unexpected situations.

However, most of the crippling effects of fear that limit people on a daily basis fall under the heading of uncertainty. I call it the "what if syndrome". What is the 'what if syndrome'? What if syndrome is the negative mind-set being expressed in a future tense. Since the mind is only creative, this is an extremely dangerous way to protect your energy. It can easily become a self-fulfilling prophecy. This is true even if you have thought something like "I don't think I can do it. I don't want people to laugh at me. What if I fail? You have to change this". What you are really projecting is something negative which means you are afraid. So right away, your creative mind goes to work. Looking for a way to manifest the very result you are fearful of. What can you do? You have to change your focus. The obvious solution here is to stop projecting fear into your future. I will suggest a twofold approach.

Number one, you need to shift your focus in a much more positive direction. Number two, it's a good idea to identify things that encourage feelings of insecurity and eliminate them from your life.

This second step can have a huge impact on your overall outlook. For you to be able to achieve all that which you want to achieve in life, you have to learn to do it afraid. Successful people don't give up. When you are faced with situations, you have to learn to deal with it. See it as a major challenge which you have to fight to stand still. In life, your subconscious mind will always crop up especially when you want to do something positive. The way you fight your subconscious mind determines the outcome you will get. If you refuse to do it afraid, you will remain where you are.

So many people die with their dreams because they don't know how to do it afraid. They want to wait for the right opportunity to come. And when the opportunity comes, they won't even know that is the opportunity. If you say you don't want to do it because people will ridicule you if you fail, anyhow you look at it, people will still ridicule you. Those who did it well, people still ridiculed them. So what are you scared of? Don't let people's criticism stop you from doing what you want to do. You are not a failure. If you hold that tightly, and you work positively by doing it afraid, you will accomplish your mission.

CHAPTER 5

TURNING YOUR PROBLEMS INTO OPPORTUNITIES

One of the most insidious and unproductive ways we spend our time is complaining about our problem especially when we should see it as a challenge which we can turn to our advantage. Have you got a problem? Great! In problems, there are lots of opportunities. In fact, one of the greatest attributes of a successful person is the ability to turn problems into opportunities. I will like to share a story with you. *A long time ago, there were two friends who were working in the same company. Their names were Mark and Alan. They got to the office one morning and they were invited into the office of their chairman. The chairman looked at both of them and said, "Both of you have been with us for the past six years, I am sorry to inform you that your services are no longer needed in this organisation". Their appointment was terminated. They both left the office dejected and when they got home, they prepared an up-to-date C.V and started job hunting again. They moved from one office to the other looking for job. Week ran into weeks and month to months. One day, Alan called Mark "I think I need a break; we have been moving around for a while looking for job without getting any". He went back to his old ways of drinking, smoking and hanging out with wrong friends while Mark continued searching for job. He dropped his CV with different companies.*

One day, as Mark was moving around he got into a company and he was fortunate to meet the owner of that company. The owner of the company said to him "young man I have gone through your CV. You have vast experience but it's so unfortunate that we don't have any vacant position for the kind of job you are looking for. The only position we have is that of a volunteer. We need someone that can help on a voluntary basis and we are ready to pay the person little money on a weekly basis. Because Mark had been out of job for a long time and he needed some money, he agreed to take the voluntary position. Few weeks later, one of the directors in the company died, then the Owner of the company invited Mark into his office and gave him the position of a director from the voluntary position he held before. He was given a house, an official car and a good salary.

TURNING YOUR PROBLEMS INTO OPPORTUNITIES

Think about this; how do you see your problem? Do you see your problem as a problem or do you see your problem as a challenge which you can turn around to your advantage? Complaining about your problem will not give you the solution. Mourning to people about your problem will not give you the desired result. Alan saw his problem as a problem and that was why he went back to his old ways of drinking, smoking and hanging out with the wrong set of people, while Mark saw his problem as a challenge which he could turn into opportunity. He was able to turn his situation around to his advantage.

I will like to share another story with you. This is about three friends; they all wanted to go into music. Two out of the three friends came from a rich background while the third one came from a poor family. The one from a poor family was the one that seems so talented. His friends mocked him by saying "man! You have no money to go to college let alone university so how do you intend to achieve your dream of becoming a musician"? They laughed and laughed at him even though he wanted to be a musician. He did not have the necessary finance to go through college. One day, when these two friends were going for their extra moral lessons, he decided to follow them but when he got there he stood by the window and their music teacher looked at him and said, what are you doing by the window? He wanted to run away but the music teacher said no! I want you to come inside. He went into the class and sat down. The young boy watched the students as they sang one after the other. After a while, the music teacher pointed at him and asked him to come out and sing. The young boy said no! I am sorry I cannot and all the students in the class laughed at him. The teacher insisted that he should come out and sing. Reluctantly, he came out and sang. He sang so well and the teacher was impressed by his performance. At the end of the music lesson, the teacher invited him into his office and said to the young boy, "How do you see yourself? What is your ambition in Life?" The young boy said he would like to be a musician. He went on to tell the teacher that his friends said it would be difficult for him to be a musician because he does not have money to go to college or

TURNING YOUR PROBLEMS INTO OPPORTUNITIES

music school. The teacher looked at him and smiled, "you are who you think you are! You have all that is required, you have the potential, the dream is your dream. What is the problem?" The young boy said that his parents have no money to see him through college let alone university.

The teacher said, "I will take you as one of my students so you can start attending the extra moral classes.". This boy was so happy. So, he started attending the extra moral classes with his two other friends without paying any money. Few months later, his father took ill so the responsibility of caring for the family fell on him. He had to look for job to look after the Family. He went to inform the music teacher. The teacher asked him what he could do. The young boy said, "I can sing, Sir". The music teacher retorted "oh yea! I know you can sing." The teacher reached for his table and gave him one job advert. This boy looked through the advert and said "sir, they want a professional singer and I am not a professional singer". The teacher looked at him and said, "I want you to go for the position. You have got the talent and the potential of making it". The young boy tried to object but his teacher insisted. So, this young boy went there the following morning. He was invited into the hall to sing and the first question he was asked by the person conducting the interview was, "are you a singer?" The boy said "yes". Have you done this before? The boy said "No" "Are you a professional?" And he said "No" The person conducting the interview was so angry with him and he said, "young man didn't you go through the advert before coming? We said we are looking for a professional singer not someone who have not done this before. Please leave now and don't waste my time." The young boy left the hall, instead of going home, he went back to his music teacher and his teacher asked him, "What happened" The young boy said "sir, just as I envisaged, I got there and I was asked if I was a professional singer and I said No" The teacher asked him if he was able to sing for them but the boy said he was not allowed to sing.

The music teacher looked at him and said ' The interview will still be on for the next two days, I want you to go back and meet that man tomorrow and ask him to allow you to sing for him." The boy tried to object but the teacher insisted that he should go there. Unfortunately for him, when he got there the following day, he met the same man who interviewed him the previous day. On seeing him, the man conducting the interview recognised him. "Were you not the boy who came yesterday that said you have never gone through this before? What do you want again?" The young boy said he would like to sing for him and the man got angry. "Do you think we are here to play? Young boy, please leave and don't come here again." He left and went straight to his music teacher again. He told his teacher that he went back there as he advised but the man conducting the interview was so crossed with him; he even threatened to call the security to take him away if he didn't leave. The music teacher said, "In life you have to be persistent to be able to get what you are looking for. I insist, go back there the third time. Tell that man to let you sing for him because I see in you the potential of becoming a good singer."

We all have this subconscious mind that tells us things especially when you want to do something positive, that your subconscious mind will start telling you "you can't do it! It's not for you" The next day as this young boy dressed up to go back to the place, his subconscious mind started telling him not to forget what he was told by the man at the interview that he was going to call security to get him out of the building. Why do you want to go there and ridicule yourself? You are not a professional singer so stay back! However, this boy was able to fight his subconscious mind. He went there. It was still the same man he had met those two other days that was still there conducting the interview. This time, the man conducting the interview got furious and said "young man it is obvious that you are looking for trouble you have been here twice and I told you that we don't need you because we are looking for a professional". The boy became aggressive as well and said "I insist, let me sing for you. You have been allowing other people to sing and I want to sing as well. Wouldn't you have allowed me to sing if I had lied to you?" Because this young boy was courageous, the man conducting the interview was shocked and he looked at him and said "ok if what you want to do is to sing, then come out and sing then leave". The boy climbed the stage sang, everyone in the hall were marvelled. They clapped for the

TURNING YOUR PROBLEMS INTO OPPORTUNITIES

young boy because he sang so well. The man conducting the interview also joined the crowd to clap for him. The boy was given the position.

This boy did not go to college because his parents could not afford to send him to school. Who are the people you have around you? Who are the people you discuss your vision with? Are they dreaming stealers? Oh yes! I call them dream stealers because they do not see what you see. You are the one with the dream. The people we discuss with matters in life. Some people will lift you up while some will run you down. You are the one with the dream so if you discuss your vision with people who think you cannot do that which you have set out to do, don't let their condemnation affect you, rather, sit back and work out how you can turn it to your advantage. Yet, he was able to make his dream of becoming a singer a reality. The young boy's dream could have died if the music Teacher had not insisted that he should persist by going after each turn down.

How do you see your problem? The fact that you didn't have the opportunity of attending college does not mean that you cannot what you have set out to achieve. The fact that you didn't have money or the opportunity of attending university doesn't mean you cannot become who you want to become.

The Young boy's friends ran him down because they told him that since he did not go to college, that there was no way he could be a Singer.

The problem of this young boy was financial. He was able to turn his financial problem to his advantage with the support of the Teacher who stood by him. This boy should also be given credit for going back each time he was asked never to come back. Some people will not go back because of fear. The boy's persistence paid off.

TURNING YOUR PROBLEMS INTO OPPORTUNITIES

You can do the same thing. What are you going through? They have told you that you cannot do it and you are now thinking, because they have said it, you cannot do it. Don't complain about your problem. Instead, look at your problem as a challenge you can turn to your advantage.

Few years ago, a client of mine called me, "sir, I will like to come and see you" and when he got to my office, he said "sir, I have got a problem." He told me that his employer just sacked him. I looked at him and smiled. I told him what I saw was not a problem but a challenge that could be turned to his advantage. "You have always dreamt of having your own company, I think this is an opportunity." But this young man looked at me and said, "I don't think that will be possible because I shared my dream with my friends and they told me I was not competent enough to own a company. I asked him if they told him the reason why they said it. His reply was, "they said I won't be able to manage people."

Who are the people around you? Who are the people you share your dream with? If you allow them to run you down, you will remain where you are, you will not be able to achieve what you want to achieve in life. I insisted that the young man shouldn't look at his problem as a problem. Rather, I advised him to work on his dream. I advised him to ignore those friends of his. I told him that he was the one that had the dream so he should work on his dream positively.

Today, this young man has his own company with over fifteen staff working for him. Think about this. How do you see yourself? Don't let people condemn you, for you can turn your situation around to your advantage. This young man was sacked; he was sacked for a reason. Oh yes! He was sacked so that he could move on in life but he did not see it that way. He was mourning about his problem. In fact, when he came to me I am sure he

TURNING YOUR PROBLEMS INTO OPPORTUNITIES

wanted me to sympathize with him and then advise him to look for another job, but I didn't see it from that perspective. Rather, I saw the potential of the young man. I advised him to go out there and do something better with his life.

Stop mourning to people about your problem, instead, see your problem as something you can turn around to your advantage.

I will like to share another story with you. This is about a young man who was going for a life changing meeting. As this man entered his car and started driving out, the petrol light came on, warning him that his car was running low on petrol. I don't know if you know this principle of E+R=O. E stands for event while R stands for your response to the event and O is the outcome. In this man's situation, his event is the light that came up warning him of his shortage of petrol, the man's response to the petrol light warning whether positive or negative will determine the outcome of the man's situation. If in this man's situation, he decided to ignore the petrol light and moved on, instead of going to the petrol station; do you know what will be his outcome? This man would stop in the middle of nowhere and he would either be late for the life changing meeting he wants to attend or he may not even be able to attend it.

How do you intend to turn your problem into opportunity, when you saw the signal and you refused to work on the signal? This man had seen the yellow light warning him of the shortage of petrol, if he did not respond positively by going to a petrol station, he would get stuck in the middle of nowhere

Most of the time, we always see signal(s), what is required is for us to take positive action to stop the situation from getting out of hand.

TURNING YOUR PROBLEMS INTO OPPORTUNITIES

How much difference can you create in your life with a subtle little shift in perception? Sometimes, the difference between the happy successful outcome and failure is only a slight shift in perception. How we represent things to ourselves determines how we will respond to any given situation, in turn, our response will help determine the response that is the E+R=O.

When life presents you with challenge, how do you feel about it? What is your initial internal response to an emotional level? What is your external response as seen through your body language and verbal expression? Why does it even matter! How we respond to any situation reveals a lot about our attitude and perception. So when we see challenges as opportunities, what does that reveal about our personal vantage point? Most likely, it means that we have a healthy degree of optimism, self-confidence and openness along with adventurous spirit. If our first response to any given situation is negative, it means a positive outcome will much more be difficult to achieve. That initial negative response will trigger our established response-pattern and we will begin to follow the innate pattern established by previous negative experiences. Some people shy away from responsibilities because it requires accountability. So let me ask you this, is it more empowering to be accountable for your own actions and attitude or to make somebody else responsible? You see, when we give away accountability, we create a situation of helplessness. So, I will encourage you to liberate yourself by accepting responsibilities. Note just that. Be 100% responsible for your actions, in that way, you will be able to take charge and people will not be able to run your life for you.

What am I talking about! I am talking about how you can turn your problems into opportunities, how you can see your problem as a challenge that you can turn to your advantage.

Look at the examples I have given you in this book, some were able to change their situations to their advantage because they did not see their problem as problem while those that could not change their situations to their advantage saw their problem as something that does not have solution. Which do you prefer, to move on in life even though you are faced with problem, or to live within the problem and allow it to drain you?

STEPS TO TURNING PROBLEMS INTO OPPORTUNITIES

- Change your language from negative to positive. View every problem in your life as a challenge or opportunity you can benefit from.

- Look into every difficulty for the seed of an equal or greater opportunity to benefit, for you will always find something good if you look for it. Look upon yourself as a professional problem solver, no matter what your job title. Continually look for better ways to solve problems and get the job done.

- Stop mourning, stop complaining to people. "Yes, you got sacked. so what?" You should look at it as something you can turn to your advantage. Do something better with your life and stop complaining. Do not go back to your old ways of drinking just because you've been sacked. The key to turning problems into solutions is if you have directed that energy away from exerting a negative influence and towards a much more positive orientation, Problem can either drain you or energize you. It all depends on the way you handle it.

For you to change a problem into opportunity, you have to get to work on it as soon as possible and don't procrastinate. A difficult problem that is avoided will not only be a problem in itself, it can also cast a negative light on everything else you do in life.

CHAPTER 6

YOU ARE NOT A FAILURE

With many disasters striking left and right, is it any wrong that you might begin to think bad things about yourself. Your boss criticises you no matter how many hours you work. You can't get everything done on time. The lover who once made you smile now always seems to harp at you. Your families are also making things worse by pointing out how you are less than perfect.

As many of you know, there are families who are much more willing to let you know that you have not lived up to their expectations. People on the street can take verbal swap at how you look and things you are not doing well. Anywhere you look, there is someone pointing out what is wrong with you. Your looks don't measure up. Your career is not where you want it to be. Relationships fall apart around you. Family is nightmare. Money is problem. Nothing is the way it is supposed to be, and people are eager to let you know that you have greatly disappointed them.

After hearing this, over and over again, so many people start to believe that they are somehow flawed. They buy into this constant peeking that trades on even those with best self-esteem. Slowly, it gets to you. And you wither inside thinking probably you are a failure. You come to think that if everyone is saying you are a failure, may be, just may be in reality you are a failure. Feeling this way can make you cringe when you look at yourself in a mirror. This can cast a shadow on everything you do in life.

Do you feel like you fail every day? As hard as you work, do you seem to get nowhere? Is it common for everything around you to go wrong? You may be fighting to keep your head above water but all you hear is criticism from others. What happens is that after a while, you begin to hear that criticism from yourself. You adopt it as your own. This little voice on the inside hunts you, telling you that you are not good enough and that you are a failure.

The more people pile on you, the worst you feel. You feel like there's something wrong with you. And you may find yourself apologising for not being good enough. You are sorry that you can't lose weight, You are sorry that your spouse had an affair, You are sorry that you haven't been able to do better at work, You are sorry that your children have done something wrong, You are sorry that you are sick and not doing well for your family, You are sorry that you married a man who beats you, You are sorry that you can't find a job. Though, you may not consider such thoughts to be harmful, thinking so little about yourself can do a lot of damage to you. Oh yes! These negative thoughts are actually hurting you.

When you internalise so much self-doubt, your body absorbs it. Your muscles will tense and inflammations will begin to wreak havoc on you and you can become sick from this. Have you ever noticed that you become ill after a very stressful time? Your body will say: "Hey! You need to take a break". This is what can happen when you allow other's negativity to affect the way you see yourself. There are a lot of demands on you. It's no wonder you can't get everything done perfectly. Who is a superman or super woman? The answer is "Nobody". There is no person on the planet earth that can satisfy everyone. It's not possible. So, allowing others to make you feel bad is something you have to avoid.

The danger of allowing it to happen to you is so great. Not only that. If you think you are a failure, the cycle will repeat itself. If you have abusive parents or spouse, have you noticed that when they criticise you, you get nervous and become more likely to mess up? If your boss is difficult, you tend to be clumsy and make mistakes. Of course, this gives people the opportunity to criticise you more. And you see yourself just the way they see you. Failure that is just all you hear and all you think about. When you accept such nonsense, you give your control away. This will make you feel even worse. In short, it will break you. No matter how many people tell you that you don't measure up, don't let that colour how you see yourself.

If you make mistakes, then you make mistakes. That doesn't mean that you are anything less than wonderful. You are not a failure. If you had a job that didn't work out, then it was a learning experience. If you stay in the negativity and let it define you, then you have been defined by something other than you. You need to define yourself. This is the only way you can find true happiness. Don't ever let anyone treat you in a way that makes you feel worthless. Think of all the good things that you've done and let those good things fill your heart. Next time you find yourself having negative thoughts, I want you to say this word: Stop! Tell yourself that you are not a failure. You deserve better. I want you to remember that. If you are reading this book, it tells me that deep down; you know that you are not a failure. All you need is a little reminder that you are someone that matter; because you need this reminder, treat yourself to something that brings smile to your face. The more you realise that you are alright, the more you will be able to do things which will bring about positive changes to your life. Never apologise for not being good enough because you are a person with value who deserves happiness. Let your spirit soar to greater heights, knowing that you are just fine. You are not a failure and you will never be one!

I will like to share a story with you. This is about a man who was frustrated that his seventeen year old son was not good enough. He decided to take him to a Zen master. This master asked him to leave his son with him for three months. And during this period, he asked the man not to visit him at all. This man complied and left his son. When it was exactly three months, the man went back to the master.

In order to convince this man, the Zen master decided to organise a karate match. It was to be between the son and some other people. All through the match, the son hardly raised his hand to hit his opponents. When he's attacked by the opponents, he would fall down only to stand up again. This happened severally. At the end of the match, this man went to the Zen master and said, "Haven't I paid you enough? You asked me to leave my son with you for three months. You haven't done anything. You didn't change him at all." Then the Zen Master said; "I am sorry that you only saw your son's inability to raise his hands to fight his opponents, didn't you notice that your son had the courage and bravery to stand up after each fall? That he could stand up when he is down, tells you that he's got the courage. He will be able to weather the storm. This man looked at the Master and said, "That's true". Then he took his son away.

What is the moral of this story?

We should not just focus on instant results when we do something. The experience gained and the efforts given are the most precious. If one's life is always smooth, then he or she will not be able to taste the final sweetness of success after many trials without giving up. That's the way it is in life. What is that thing you want to do? Are you expecting instant results? The fact that you have done it once, you have done it a few times and you didn't get it right doesn't make you a failure. The more you try the better you become.

You want to go for that job interview. Don't fill your mind with negative thoughts. See yourself as somebody that will get it. You are tall, so what? You are too short, and so? Do you think you are too fat or probably you are too slim, you are who you think you are. If you fill your mind with something positive, and work positively towards what you want to achieve, you will get it.

There is no way you will be thinking badly about yourself and expect something good. You are not a failure. Failure is painful right, but not for successful people. The most successful people in every field don't consider failure to be a painful experience because they think about it differently. Successful people transcend failure because their self-esteem, rather than depending on whether they win or lose, is based on their sense of value. Rather than taking failure seriously, they develop beliefs which allow them to capitalise upon negative feedback and turn it to their advantage.

All stories of success are also stories of great failures. But, people don't see failures. They only see one side of the picture and they say, "That person got lucky. He must have been at the right place at the right time".

I have lots of names in my list. I will share some with you. There was a man who failed in business at the age of twenty one, he was defeated in a legislative race at the age of twenty two, he failed again in business at the age of twenty four, he overcame the death of his sweet heart at the age of twenty six, he had a nervous breakdown at the age of twenty seven, he lost a congressional race at the age of thirty four, he lost a senatorial race at the age of thirty five, he failed in an effort to become vice president at the age of forty seven, he lost a senatorial race at the age of forty nine, and he was elected President of the United States at the age of fifty two. Do you know this man? This man was Abraham Lincoln. Would you call him a failure? No. He could have quit you know. But this man refused to quit because he had a dream. It's the same with all successful people. Regardless of how many times they failed, they will still continue to fight. The major difference between successful people and those who are struggling with their dream is in their persistence. The fact that you have tried it so many times and didn't get it right doesn't mean you are a failure. You will only be a failure if you quit trying.

I will like to give you another example, Oprah Winfrey. Most people know Oprah as one of the most iconic faces on T.V. as well as one of the richest and most successful women in the world. Oprah faced a hard time to get to that position. Oprah was actually sacked by her employer because they said she was not fit to appear on T.V. Oprah decided to turn this around. She worked on her weakness and she was able to do that which they said she could not do. She worked on that weakness and she was able to turn it to her advantage. You can do the same thing. You are not a failure.

Another good example is Winston Churchill. Winston Churchill was twice elected as the Prime Minister of the United Kingdom. But could you believe that Churchill actually failed the sixth grade when he was in school? After school, he faced many years of political failures as he was defeated in every election for public office. But he finally became the Prime Minister at the age of sixty two. Picture somebody who failed sixth grade. He tried severally to be elected and he failed severally. He refused to give up. He looked at himself and he said he wanted something. He worked positively towards that which he wanted.

That you are doing it or you have done it so many times and it's not working and people are mocking you, is not enough reason for you to say you want to stop trying it. If you stop trying, it will only confirm what they have said about you, that you are a failure.

Another wonderful example is Soichiro Honda. We may be familiar with Honda Motors. They are everywhere, from cars to motor cycles. But do you

YOU ARE NOT A FAILURE

know the real story of how challenging it was for Soichiro Honda to establish Honda Motors? I will tell you. Like most other countries, Japan was hit badly by the great depression of the 1930s. In 1938, Soichiro Honda was still in school when he started the little workshop developing the concept of the piston-ring. His plan was to sell this idea to Toyota. He laboured night and day. He even slept in the workshop, always believing that he could perfect the design and produce a worthy product.

At that time, he was married. When he was short of cash, he asked his wife whether he could sell her Jewellery. The wife agreed and they sold her Jewellery to continue with the design. When it was produced, he took this design to Toyota. Only for that design to be turned down because Toyota Motors said the standard was quite below their own standard. Think about this. After spending your time, your money, you sold your property to produce something because you believed that the product was going to give you something wonderful in life. It was going to be your breakthrough. You now took that product to where you are meant to supply it, only to be turned down. You are told that it was below their standard. Some people would give up.

But this man, even though he was mocked by his friends, and in debt, refused to give up. He went back to redesign the product, he then took it back again to Toyota. But this time, it was accepted because it was just exactly what they wanted. You can do the same thing. How do you see yourself? That is what I am saying about being persistent. This man refused to give up. Is that the end of the story for this man? No! I will tell you more about him. After the product had been accepted by Toyota, he was asked to supply them. So he needed a factory which he could use to supply Toyota. He decided to build a factory. He was able to gather materials

65

together and built the factory. Upon completing the factory, do you know what happened to this man? He was faced with another situation; a very strong problem, because this factory was burnt twice. It's enough for anybody to say, "You know what, I think this is enough for me". This man refused to quit. He continued and he said to himself he was going to do it. Do you know why this man refused to quit? It is because he believed so much in himself. He did not let the distractions of the naysayers to stop him from working on his dream.

In life, people dream and they want something good. They want to work towards who they want to be or what they want in life. But when they are faced with situations, they give up. There is no way one can avoid facing problems in life, especially when you are working on the road to success. As you are working to get something done, you will face obstacles, you will face problem, you will face situations. The way you handle your problem will determine the outcome you will get. This man refused to give up. Soichiro Honda started collecting surplus gasoline can discarded by U.S fighters who were fighting wars at that time. This was what he used to build the new factory. After the war, an extreme gasoline shortage forced people to walk or use bicycle. Honda built a fighting engine and attached it to his bicycle. His neighbours wanted the same thing. Although he tried, materials could not be found and he was unable to supply his neighbours. Was it the end of the road for him? No! Soichiro refused to give up.

He wrote inspiring letters to eighteen thousand shops of bicycle owners, asking them to help him revitalise Japan. Five thousand people responded by giving him money to support his ideas. Unfortunately for him, the first models were too bulky to work well. So he continued to develop and adapt until finally the small engine which he named "Super Cub", became a reality

YOU ARE NOT A FAILURE

and was a success. With success in Japan, Honda began exporting his bicycle engines to Europe and America.

Was that the end of the story? No! In the 1970s, there was another gas shortage. This time in America, automotive fashion turned to small cars. Honda was paid to be on the trend because they were now experts in building small engine cars. The companies started making tiny cars smaller than anyone had ever seen before, and rode another wave of success. Today, Honda Corporation employed over hundred thousand people in the U.S.A. and Japan. And it's one of the world's largest automobile companies.

Honda succeeded because one man made a truly committed decision, acted upon it and made adjustment on a continuous basis. Failure was simply not considered a possibility. You can do the same thing. What are you planning to do? When you are faced with problems, People will ridicule you, they will mock you, and they will tell you that you cannot do it. But how do you see yourself? Do you see yourself as somebody who will be able to achieve what you have set out to achieve? Or do you see yourself as a failure that they call you? It is even good for them to call you a failure; and for you to work around it and turn it to your advantage. Look at all the names I have mentioned in this book.

Oprah was condemned. She was sacked because her employer said she was not fit to appear on T.V. Oprah was able to change things around to her advantage. Today, we know her to be very successful for her Television programme. Look at Soichiro. He faced so many problems. He committed his time. He sold his properties; he even went ahead to pawn his wife's jewelleries just to achieve what he had set out to achieve. Imagine going out to borrow money to build a factory and it got burnt twice? Not only that. He looked for money again; he built another factory, only to be taken away by earthquake. All these are enough reasons for any man to say he wants to give up. Some people don't even face this much problems before they give up in life. This man refused to give up because he was so sure of himself. He didn't see giving up as an option.

Look at Winston Churchill, He tried so many times to be elected into a public office but he failed. This man refused to give up. You can do the same thing. You are not a failure. Don't even consider being a failure, because you are not. For you to be able to achieve what you want to achieve, you must be able to take the bull by the horn. Let people run their mouth. They will talk. Some will lift you up; some will try to bring you down. You are hundred per cent responsible for your actions in life. You have to take charge.

Don't see yourself the way they see you. If they condemn you and you decide to live with that condemnation, then you are a condemned person. It is best for you not to flow with that condemnation and work positively towards getting that which you want to achieve. Don't allow their condemnation to affect you.

Long time ago, there was a man who joined a company as a sales representative. Few months later there was vacancy within the company. He went to his friend and said he would like to apply for the vacancy. His friend looked at him and said, you only just joined this company. You will not be able to cope. There is no point in you trying at all. Because this young man knew what he wanted for himself in life, he knew he could do it. He didn't listen to this friend of his. He went to another friend and discussed the same issue with him. This other friend looked at him and said; "I think you have the experience. Go for that job". This man decided to listen to his second friend because he wanted that job. He worked positively towards getting that job. He submitted his C.V. and he was called for interview and eventually, he got that job. Picture that!

Who are the people you have around you? Some people will try to lift you up. Some will bring you down. It is now up to you to take action. It is not a bad thing for you to ask people questions or share your dream and vision with people, but it will be so easy for you to know whether they share the same vision. If they run you down, don't blame them. Just move on. Walk away from them. Sit back and think about how you want to do your thing. You are in charge. Don't go around blaming people for what you have done or what you refused to do. Some will say, "Oh! I wouldn't have done that, but for the wrong advice I got from my friend". Don't blame your father. Don't blame your mum or your sister. You are to be blamed for whatever happened to you in life. If you don't take charge of your life, people will run your life for you.

You are not a failure. You will not be a failure for failing so many times to achieve something. You will only be a failure if you quit trying, and that is the major difference between those who are successful and those who could not make it. When you are faced with problems, and the first thing that comes to mind is to quit, how do you intend to win? How do you intend to achieve that which you have set out to achieve when you fill your mind with negative thoughts? Change your reasoning, change that thought from something negative to something positive and work positively towards that which you want to get.

One of the biggest things that people do that set them up for failure is that they make excuses. By saying that you don't have time or you don't know how, you are just using excuses to shy away from something you think you may fail at. How will you know if you will be able to get it if you don't make the move? Setting yourself up for success will not guarantee that you will get everything you want without failure, but it will definitely make your journey easier to travel and help you find your way. Failure is the other side of success and without it there could be no joy in pushing through.

What am I talking about here? Persistence! Persistence is the source of success for the majority of people on this planet. Overnight successes are rare. Lack of persistence is the major reason as to why many people fail. Giving up too soon means that you will never know whether you will be able to achieve what you have set out to achieve.

Collins Adams at the age of sixty five, with a beetle car and a hundred dollar cheque from social security, realised that he had to do something. He remembered his mother's recipe and went out selling. It was estimated that he had knocked on more than a thousand doors before he got his first order. How many of us quit after three trials, ten trials or a hundred trials. And then we say we have tried as hard as we could.

As a young cartoonist, World Disney faced many rejections from newspaper editors as well. They said he did not have the talent. Disney worked on himself and he was able to do that which they said he could not do.

I will like to share another great story with you. One day, a partially deaf four year old kid came home from school with a note from his teacher: "Your Tommy is too stupid to learn, get him out of school". His mother read the note and answered; "My Tommy is not stupid to learn, I will teach him myself". And that Tommy grew up to be the great Thomas Edison. Thomas Edison had only three months of formal schooling, and he was partially deaf. In case you don't know Thomas Edison, he was the one who made light bulb. This man didn't fail there alone. He tried so many times before he was able. In fact, he actually tried approximately nine hundred and ninety-nine times before he was able to make that light bulb that we use today. You can do the same thing. Just because they say you are a failure doesn't make you a failure. Successful people don't give up. They keep doing things until they are able to achieve what they want to achieve.

CHAPTER 7

YOU ARE WHO YOU THINK YOU ARE

All of us have a voice which talks to us, you might think of it as your conscience. It might be that inner observer who seems to sit in the corner and watches everything you do. You may recognise it as that voice that starts talking to you upon your awakening in the morning. Sometimes, it may wait until you look at yourself in the mirror before it actually speaks to you. It is that voice which tells you that you are beautiful, you are handsome, what a wonderful person you are, you are going to have a great day, and you are so slim and got a right figure. If you don't recognise that voice, then it may be speaking to you in a different tone. Probably what you are hearing or you are seeing is something negative , you may be hearing things like "you look like crab today, you have sure gained a lot of weight, your hair is a mess, it is a terrible day, common get back to bed".

This voice, the negative critical one, is one of the main reasons why so many people have problems. It can destroy resilience about opening the flood gate and draining away your energy. This voice can make everything you do go wrong. You may be like most people who know how to take small problem, think about it for a while, and then it becomes a bigger one. That little voice keeps telling you what might go wrong. All of those possibilities are pointed out to you; the imagination creates a very bad situation. The problem got from a mild annoyance to a major catastrophe as you convince yourself that the imagined situation is the real situation. You are now busy confronting a problem which only exists in your mind. Any response at this point is going to be out of proportion to the original problem. The normal reaction to the original problem is most likely some degree of emotional distress. You have been laid off from a job, you may be feeling tensed, worried, anxious, sad, irritated, frustrated or angry and all of these are normal emotion for this experience. However, that inner voice may be telling you something else.

The voice could be exaggerating your situation. Probably what you are hearing is horrible and terrible. You could be hearing things like: "you will never find another job, you are a hopeless and helpless person, no one will ever hire you, you won't be able to pay your bills, you will lose everything you have and you just have to give up". With such a running dialogue, you will soon fall into depression or become enraged at your imagined maltreatment.

In a deep depression you may decide that the situation is hopeless and become suicidal. In a state of rage, you may act in an inappropriate manner towards your former employer. Either reaction is too intense; because the response is to a situation you have created in your mind. Change your mind, your attitude and your problem will shrink back to where it came from originally. The original problem may be bad enough but it's not the catastrophe you have invented. You are responsible for your thinking. Change your thinking and life will get better. But what thought do you change? Your troublesome thought about your situation can easily be found in your self-talk.

What is self-talk?

Self-talk is that inner running dialogue you have within you. It is that mind that is telling you about life situation. To change your attitude, you must change your dialogue, to change the dialogue you must catch it in action, to do this you have to pay attention to yourself. You must engage in self-observation and listen to that inner voice that keeps talking to you. What is your inner voice saying to you? It could be telling you something positive or something negative anyhow. The next time you find yourself feeling bad don't start asking who did this to me. Don't start looking around for external cause of your problems. What I will advise you do is to ask yourself "what have I been thinking? What have I been telling myself?" You will find out that your inner dialogue has put you deep into emotional distress. We are creatures of habit. We tend to follow the pictures in our mind created by our parent or neighbourhood, our towns and parts of the world from which we come from for good or for bad. But we don't have to. We need to have a mind of our own capable of imagining life the way we want to. I will advise you to start imagining life the way you want to. Create a picture in your mind and think about that picture steadfastly all day long. I want you to believe in that picture which you have created, you don't have to tell anybody about it. Have your own quiet confidence that you can make the picture in your mind come true. You will start making different choices in line with your picture; you will take small step in the right direction. As you do this, be ready to face situations, circumstances and obstacles. When you are faced with such, be ready to fight it to stand- still.

Our thought process can have a dramatic impact on our everyday life and more often than not, they are not correct. If you find out that you think negatively about yourself try to act the opposite way. For instance, instead Of thinking that you are useless, look at yourself as somebody responsible. Instead of thinking about things you cannot do, look at it in a positive way and start saying, "I can do it" Believe in it that you can do it, and take positive action towards getting it done. We are usually what we think! Our character is a complete sum up of all our thoughts. As a plant springs out from the seed so every act of us spring from the hidden seeds of our thoughts and could not have appeared without them, we are made or unmade by ourselves. By the right choice and application of thought we rise to the highest mountains. By the abuse and wrong use of thoughts we fall below the lowest level of the game and we are always the master and maker. This probably is the greatest discovery throughout all of human history, that

YOU ARE WHO YOU THINK YOU ARE

we are the master of thoughts, the moulders of character, the maker and shaper of condition, environment and destiny.

I will like to share a story with you; this is about not giving up easily. If you are familiar with success book, titled, "Think and grow rich", you might remember the story in that book about a man who gave up his quest for gold too soon during the California gold rush long ago. The story goes like this: From months upon months this man went about prospecting for gold in hills. Somehow he just knew that he will strike gold. Every day he got up early and walked to the hills in search of his fortune. He dug and dug with his simple tool, he found gold here and there but never anything to write home about. The story goes that he finally gave up digging because he could not find the mother gold he was searching for.

Hearing this, another prospector came to him and offer to buy all the tools he's got. The man agreed and sold his tools for whatever money he would get for them. This prospector then went on to hire a land surveyor and engineers and geologist and they all combined their knowledge and went to work on the land which the first man had been digging before without result. It was told that upon studying the area and the mine, the men discovered that the first man had been literally three feet from where he would have reached the gold he wanted.

Literally three feet! This poor prospector who had given up was so close to the gold, he could reach and touch it but there was no way he could know this because he gave up too soon and did not take the proper tools for this job. Picture that! Imagine somebody who woke up in the morning and decided he was going to go after something. He tried for weeks; weeks ran into month and month into months when he was about to get that which he had longed for, he gave up.

The major difference between those who could not make it and those who made it, is the fact that, those who made it refused to give up and just like this man who gave up, those who could not make it, quit trying. This man would have been able to achieve what he had set out to achieve. He only laboured in vain because all that which he did, somebody came and benefited from it.

What exactly am I talking about? I am saying that you are who you think you are. I will like to share another story with you.

One day a farmer's donkey fell into a well. The animal cried desperately for hours and the farmer tried to figure out what he could do to bring out the animal from the well. Finally after much trial, he decided to let go, he gave up. So he invited all his neighbours to come over and help him. Everyone grabbed a shovel and began to shovel dirt into the well. At first, the donkey realised what was happening and cried horribly, and then to everyone's amazement he quieted down. A few minutes later, the farmer looked down the well just to see what was happening; he was astonished at what he saw. With each shovel of dirt that hit the back of the animal, the donkey was doing something amazing, he would shake it off and step up. Picture that! As the farmer's neighbours continued to shovel dirt on top of the animal it would shake it off and take a step up. Pretty soon, everyone was amazed as the donkey stepped over the edge of the well and happily trotted off.

What is the moral of this story?

Life is going to shovel all kinds of dirt on you. The trick of getting out of the well is to shake it off and take a step up.

Each of our trouble is a stepping stone. You can get out of the deepest well just by not stopping, never giving up, shaking it off and taking a step up.

YOU ARE WHO YOU THINK YOU ARE

What is that thing that is causing you depression? You can only solve your problems by thinking positively. If you continue to bombard yourself with negative thoughts, you will not be able to achieve what you have set out to achieve.

Another thing is about the people you have around you, what are they telling you? Are they lifting you up or bringing you down? Whatever it is, you are hundred per cent responsible for the actions you take. You are who you think you are. If you see yourself as somebody who can get that position, you will get it. You can't just get it by saying "yes, I want to get it". Rather, you will get it if you work positively towards getting it. But if you fill your mind with something negative, probably what you are thinking is; "Oh! I don't think I will be able to get it" .Do you think with this negative thought you will be able to get it even if it is given to you on a platter of gold? No! It will be so difficult. You have to change your reasoning now, for you to be able to get that which you want to get in life.

If you see yourself as a failure, then you will remain a failure. If people around you say you cannot get something, you can change it around to your advantage. That man who was digging for gold would have been smiling but he gave up too soon. Don't give up. Successful people don't quit.

I will like to share another story with you. This is about a young boy who was called Sparky by his uncle. This young boy failed every subject in his eighth grade. He failed physics in the high school getting a grade of zero. He also failed Latin, Algebra and English and his record in sport wasn't anything better. Though, he managed to be in the school's golf team, he promptly lost the only important match of the season. Oh! There was a consolation match and he lost that too. Throughout his youth, Sparky was awkward socially. It was not that people did not want to play with him but he just didn't know how to relate with people. Sparky was a loser. He, his classmates and everyone knew it. So he learnt to live with it. He made up his mind early that if things were meant to work out, they would, otherwise, he would be satisfied with what appear to be his inevitable mediocrity. One thing was important to Sparky though, drawing! In his senior year of high school, he submitted some cartoons to the year book, the editors rejected the concept. Do you know why? They did not bother to check his art work. They refused to check the art work because it was from sparky. They have known sparky to be a failure. They think it was a waste of time going through the cartoon he had submitted to them. Despite this brush off, sparky was convinced of his ability. He even decided to become an artist. Imagine somebody who submitted to an editor and his cartoon was rejected. Instead of feeling bad about himself, he decided that he was going to change the whole thing around to his advantage. He worked on his weakness.

After completing high school, sparky wrote World Disney Studio. They asked for his sample art works. Despite careful preparation, the art works which he presented to them was rejected as well but sparky still did not give up. Instead, he decided to tell his own life story in cartoons. The main character would be a little boy who symbolised a perpetual loser and chronic under-achiever. You know him well because sparky's cartoon character went on to become a cultural phenomenon of sorts.

People readily identified with this and they called it lovable loser. The cartoon reminded people of the painful and embarrassing moment from their own past. It reminded them of their pain and shared humanity. Sparky's story reminded us of a very important principle of life. We all face difficulties and discouragements from time to time but we also have choice of how we handle them. If we are persistent, if we hold fast to our belief and work positively towards what we want to achieve, we will get it. Look at Sparky in this story, because he failed to do something well, he was tagged a failure by his friends and people around him.

How do you see yourself? Because you could not do something right and people looked down on you does not mean you have to look down on yourself. Sparky refused to see himself as a failure; he worked on his weakness and was able to change the whole thing around to his advantage. Sparky became successful because he did not let people's condemnation affect his reasoning. What am I talking about? You are who you think you are. Just because your friends said you cannot do it does not mean you cannot do it. You will only be unable to do it, if you don't put in your best. If you have a dream and you want to work positively towards achieving your dream along the way, you will meet so many people. The way you relate with people and the way you handle situation will determine the outcome you will get. If you are such that give up easily then you will not be able to achieve what you have set out to achieve.

If you are going to be successful in creating a life of your dream, you have to believe that you are capable of making it happen. You have to believe that you have the right stuff, that you are able to do it. Another thing you have to learn to do is to give up the phrase: I can't, it's not possible and all its cousins such as: I wish I was able to. The word "I can't" actually disempowers you. If you fill your mind with something negative you will not be able to think positively towards getting that which you have set out to achieve. Change the "I can't "to "I can", the" it's not possible" to "it is possible", I will get it.

You are who you are today because of your past actions, probably you decided not to do something positively. You had a dream, instead of working positively towards achieving your dream; you decided not to take action. You decided to fill your mind with negative thoughts. Once you know your life's purpose, determine your vision and clarify what you truly want for yourself. What do you desire? You have to convert them into measurable goals and objectives and then act on them positively with the correct mind-set that you will achieve them.

Change your reasoning and everything around you will change.

You are not a failure for trying so many times to achieve something. You will only be a failure if you quit trying. Learn to DO IT AFRAID.

NOTES

NOTES

NOTES

NOTES

NOTES

NOTES

www.ingramcontent.com/pod-product-compliance
Lightning Source LLC
Chambersburg PA
CBHW072232170526
45158CB00002BA/858